1621

A NEW LOOK AT

Thanksgiving

CATHERINE O'NEILL GRACE and MARGARET M. BRUCHAC
With PLIMOTH PLANTATION

Photographs by SISSE BRIMBERG and COTTON COULSON

SCHOLASTIC INC.
New York Toronto London Auckland Sydney
Mexico City New Delhi Hong Kong Buenos Aires

1621
A NEW LOOK AT
Thanksgiving

Table of Contents

BACKGROUND: *View of a smoke hole in a wetu, a Native home.*

Foreword

NANCY BRENNAN, EXECUTIVE DIRECTOR, PLIMOTH PLANTATION
MARGARET M. BRUCHAC,
WAMPANOAG INDIAN PROGRAM ADVISORY COMMITTEE

BACK IN THE 19TH CENTURY, one paragraph of only 115 words in one letter written in 1621 about a harvest gathering inspired the growth of an American tradition that became a national holiday: Thanksgiving. A number of today's assumptions about that event are based more on fiction than on fact. Many Americans think that the Pilgrims took over empty land from roving Native wanderers who had no fixed settlement. They are unaware of the continued existence of Native people. Unquestioning acceptance of biased interpretations can affect the way we treat one another, even today.

In 1947 the founders of Plimoth Plantation created a museum to honor the 17th-century English colonists who would come to be known to the world as the Pilgrims. In doing so, the founders left out the perspective of the Wampanoag people who had lived on the land for thousands of years. At Plimoth Plantation today, we ask questions about what really happened in the past. We draw from the new research of scholars who study documents, artifacts, homesites, culture, and formerly untapped sources such as the Wampanoag people themselves. We encourage new scholarship that includes multiple perspectives.

What you will read in these pages represents new thinking about the people and events of 1621. This book is just one part of a museum-wide effort to reinterpret the 1621 harvest feast, through books, videos, educational materials, and a reenactment that gave birth to these photographs. We invite you to join us here on this shore and view the past from a different perspective.

Two interpreters—trained role players who portray 17th-century people— pause to talk at Plimoth Plantation, a living-history museum in Massachusetts.

A BOUNTIFUL HARVEST

B Y THE ENGLISH CALENDAR, it is autumn 1621. For the Wampanoag, it is *Keepunumuk,* the time of the harvest. In a small settlement on the edge of the sea, more than 90 Native men, members of the Wampanoag Nation, share food with 52 English people. The English are survivors of the 101 who arrived less than a year earlier aboard a ship called *Mayflower.* For more than 12,000 years, Native people have fished these waters, hunted these woods, and cultivated these fields. The Wampanoag know this village site as Patuxet. The English have renamed it New Plymouth.

When the English landed in the Wampanoag homeland, Patuxet was empty because the population of the village had been devastated by plague. During their first winter, more than half of the English died. Now, in autumn, the survivors are celebrating their first successful harvest. Massasoit, a Wampanoag *sachem,* or leader, who has kept close watch on these strangers, has arrived with 90 of his warriors. For three days, this group, both English and Wampanoag, will eat together and engage in diplomacy.

Over the centuries, the story of this event will be lost, recovered, told, and retold. Traditions and misunderstandings will turn the so-called First Thanksgiving into an American popular myth, not a true story. Generations of schoolchildren have imagined brave, peaceful settlers—the "Pilgrims"—inviting a few wild Indians over for dinner. In the myth, the Wampanoag side has been left out. The true story is a lot more complicated.

History is never simple. The history of the English colonies in America is a history of European people imposing their culture, politics, and religion onto Native people. It is also a litany of the voices of many Natives, both past and present, who have persisted through plagues, war, and invasion. Read, listen, and think about this, our shared history.

Native harvests varied from season to season. Wampanoag people grew corn and other vegetables in gardens and gathered nuts, berries, and other wild plant foods. They also hunted game and caught fish in both fresh and salt water.

PEOPLE OF THE FIRST LIGHT

*T*HE WORD "Wampanoag" means "People of the Light," though the Wampanoag have come to be known as the "People of the First Light" or "People of the East." The Wampanoag Indian Program at Plimoth Plantation is dedicated to preserving their history. Nanepashemet, the former director of the program, wrote of his people: "We are the first people to see the beginning of the day. We traditionally refer to ourselves as...the People, implying original, common people. We are the true People of this land, what is now called southeastern Massachusetts and eastern Rhode Island. We have lived with this land for thousands of generations, fishing in the waters, planting and harvesting crops, hunting the four-legged and winged beings and giving respect and thanks for each and every thing taken for our use. We were originally taught to use many resources, remembering to use them with care, respect and a mind toward preserving some for seven generations of unborn and not to waste anything."

Wampanoag people gathered an abundance of food from the sea, including mussels, clams, and fish. Today, quahaugs (hard-shelled clams) are still an important food source, and their shells are made into wampum beads.

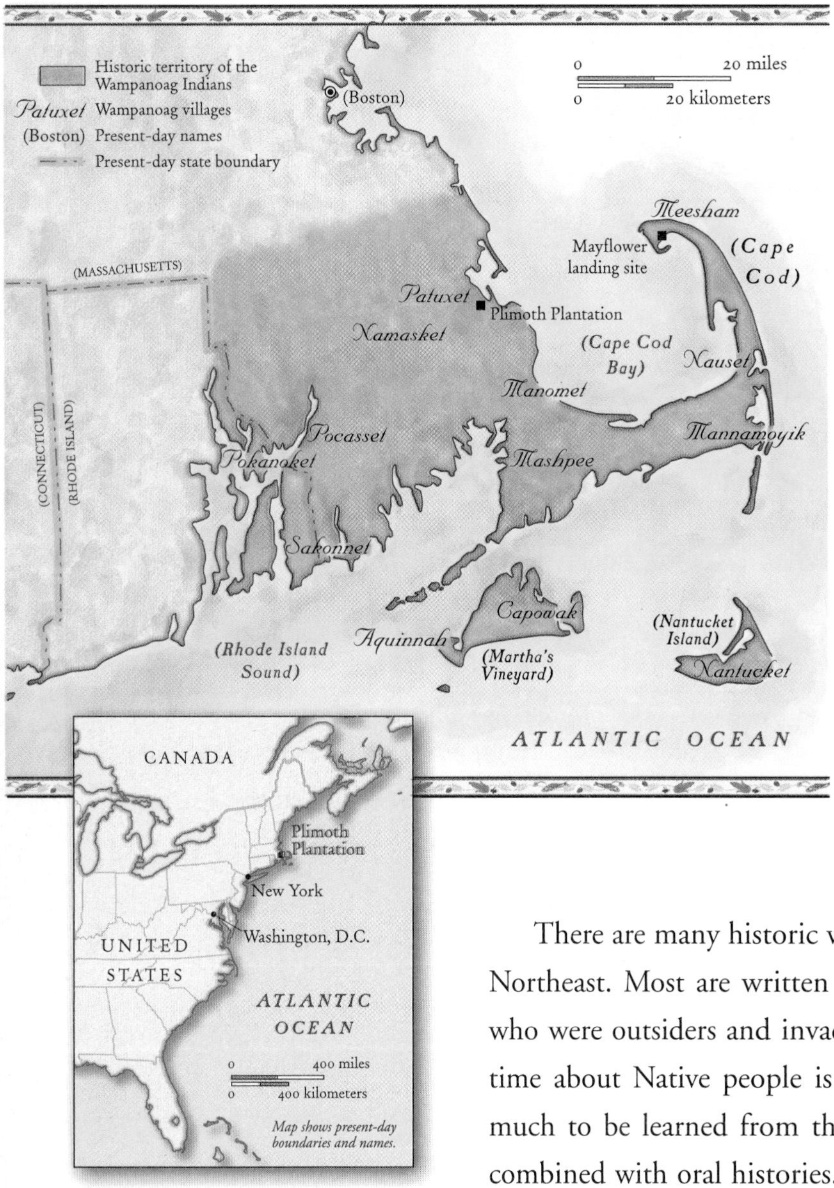
Historic territory of the Wampanoag Indians
Patuxet Wampanoag villages
(Boston) Present-day names
Present-day state boundary
0 20 miles
0 20 kilometers
(Boston)
Meesham
Mayflower landing site
(Cape Cod)
(MASSACHUSETTS)
Patuxet
Plimoth Plantation
Namasket
(Cape Cod Bay)
Nauset
Manomet
Pocasset
Pokanoket
Mashpee
Mannamoyik
(CONNECTICUT)
(RHODE ISLAND)
Sakonnet
Capowak
Aquinnah
(Martha's Vineyard)
(Nantucket Island)
Nantucket
(Rhode Island Sound)
ATLANTIC OCEAN
CANADA
Plimoth Plantation
New York
Washington, D.C.
UNITED STATES
ATLANTIC OCEAN
0 400 miles
0 400 kilometers
Map shows present-day boundaries and names.

In the 17th century, Wampanoag territory extended from Grafton, Massachusetts, to the southeastern corner of Rhode Island, and across Cape Cod, including the islands now called Martha's Vineyard and Nantucket. All Wampanoag people knew the boundaries of this territory. They considered themselves caretakers of this land. It was owned by none, but held and used with respect by all. Wampanoag life centered on providing food and shelter for families and maintaining peaceful villages. Councils of elders, clan leaders, and chiefs called *sachems* led the People and worked to keep families, villages, and the Wampanoag Nation strong.

There are many historic writings about the Native people of the Northeast. Most are written from the point of view of Europeans who were outsiders and invaders. Much of what was written at the time about Native people is wrong or distorted. But there is still much to be learned from these writings, especially when they are combined with oral histories. The oral histories of the Wampanoag people—the spoken words that have been passed on from generation to generation for thousands of years—have continued into the present. Valuable lessons are always learned from the retelling of past events and traditional stories. Such retelling also helps keep a culture and community alive and connected.

A man stands with his son by a nighttime fire. Wampanoag traditions are passed on from the old to the young through stories that speak of the ancestors and strengthen connections to the land.

Wampanoag Language

THE WAMPANOAG LANGUAGE, correctly spelled Wôpanâak, is one of a family of related languages that springs from a time, thousands of years past, when all the People of this continent's eastern region spoke one original language.

Wôpanâak language combines sounds and relationships into long words—one Wampanoag word is often a whole sentence in English. Early European colonists who listened to spoken Wôpanâak, with its many syllables, described it as sounding like a rippling brook. Some Wôpanâak words are known to speakers of English today. For example, the modern dish of corn and beans called "succotash" came from the Wampanoag word "sukahtash."

The language also reflects the philosophy that all people in the Nation are connected. When Wampanoag people speak about relatives, for example, each kinship term uses certain syllables to specify the relationship of the relative to both the speaker and the listener.

Many Wampanoag were quicker to learn English than the English were to speak Wôpanâak. In the 17th century, a written form of the language was created. The first bible printed in the New World was in Wôpanâak: missionary John Eliot's version of the King James Bible, translated in 1663 by two English-speaking Natives.

By the mid-1800s, however, English assimilation efforts led to the gradual decline of Wôpanâak. Today, some of the same documents the English used to convert the Wampanoag are helping Wampanoag people remember their original language.

Mats of woven bulrush hold the heat of the fire in the wetu
(Native home) as a family shares a meal.

COLONIZING THE NEW WORLD

$\mathcal{T}$HE *MAYFLOWER* VOYAGERS were not the first explorers in Wampanoag territory. English, Dutch, and French explorers, fisherman, and traders were here many years before *Mayflower*. It was not unusual for Europeans to kidnap Native people as curiosities. In the early 1600s English traders kidnapped at least 29 Wampanoag men, who were held in Europe for years and who learned the language and observed the ways of the English.

The early European visitors to North America brought trade. But they also brought sickness. The Wampanoag people had no resistance to these new diseases. From 1616 to 1618 a plague swept the coast from what is now Maine to Massachusetts, killing so many Native people that in some places there were not enough healthy people to bury the dead. In Patuxet, a Wampanoag village on Plymouth Harbor, so many people died that the village was abandoned.

An Englishman carries water through the streets of Plymouth using a yoke and buckets. The colony had many springs. ABOVE: By the fall of 1621, there were seven dwelling houses in the town.

The origins of the Plymouth Colony were in a congregation of English Protestants, called Separatists, who had broken away from the dominant Church of England. They lived in exile in Leiden, Holland. After a dozen years of economic hardship in Holland, this English congregation decided to seek a new home. They received funding from some English merchants to sail across the Atlantic to find a place to settle in the New World.

After several lengthy delays, a total of 101 men, women, and children set sail from Plymouth, England, on September 6, 1620. On board the ship, members of the Holland congregation were joined by other Englishmen. During the voyage, one baby was born and one passenger died. The ship reached land on November 11 after 66 days at sea.

The region and harbor where *Mayflower* landed were called Cape Cod by English sailors and fishermen. The English colonists had not planned to arrive there at all. They had intended to land at the mouth of the Hudson River, where New York City now stands, but contrary winds kept them from rounding Cape Cod to travel southward. Because winter was approaching, they decided to find a nearby place to stay.

For a month, the English explored the territory. They discovered, and stole, Wampanoag supplies: corn from storage pits, beads and ornaments from gravesites, and baskets and pots from the Native homes called *wetus*. One colonist wrote: "Whilst some of us were digging up this, some others found another heap of corn, which they digged up also, so as we had in all about ten bushels, which will serve us sufficiently for seed. And sure it was God's good providence that we found this corn, for else we know not how we should have done, for we knew not how we should find or meet with any Indians, except it be to

An Englishman fires his musket, used for hunting as well as defense. The musket was fired when the burning match (cord) was brought in contact with the prime (gunpowder).

In 1621 the majority of the colonists in the village were men.

do us a mischief." The colonists thought they had a right to help themselves to whatever they pleased. They believed God had provided the supplies for their use. The Wampanoag thought these English were behaving like disrespectful thieves.

Using a small working boat, the English continued to explore the bay, looking for a good place to set up their colony. At one point in their exploration, a storm blew them into Plymouth harbor. They thought that this place was suitable for their needs and decided to settle there. English explorer John Smith had already named this location New Plymouth, after a town in England. What the colonists found around New Plymouth was not an empty wilderness, though it may have looked so to their English eyes. It was Patuxet, which still had tilled fields, homesites, graves, trails, and food stores.

On December 25, the English started building homes at the place they now called Plymouth. The English believed that any "unimproved" or wild land was the rightful property of Christian Europeans. In a letter to his financial backers in England, Robert Cushman wrote of the Native people: "Their land is spacious and void, and there are few…They are not industrious, neither have art, science, skill or faculty to use either the land or the commodities of it, but all spoils, rots, and is marred for want of manuring, gathering, ordering, etc...so is it lawful now to take a land which none useth, and make use of it." But the English didn't understand what they were looking at. The land was far from empty and chaotic. It had been inhabited, tilled, and traveled by Native people for thousands of years. It just didn't look like Europe.

The English brought their own clothes, furniture, seeds, and other goods along with them on their journey, hoping to create a "new" England.

WAMPANOAG DIPLOMACY

On March 16, 1621, the English had a surprise visit from Samoset, a leader from the Abenaki people to the north. He stayed for several days, amazing them because he could speak English. One of the colonists wrote: "He was a man free in speech, so far as he could express his mind, and of a seemly carriage....He had a bow and two arrows, the one headed, and the other unheaded."

Samoset was there to gather information. His two arrows, one blunt and one pointed, most likely carried a message: Will it be peace or war with these strangers? Samoset brought Tisquantum (often called Squanto), one of the Wampanoag men who had been kidnapped by earlier English explorers. Tisquantum had returned to his homeland only to find that he was one of the last surviving people from Patuxet village. Tisquantum agreed to live among the colonists and act as a translator. Another Wampanoag *pniese,* or warrior-councilor,

---

This man is a pniese, *one of many who accompanied Massasoit when he visited the English at Plymouth.*
ABOVE: Painted detail of a deerskin mantle.

Hobbamock, also moved his family to the site to keep an eye on the settlement.

Diplomatic meetings, held at Plymouth, were arranged between Massasoit and the English governor, John Carver. They made a formal agreement including rules for contact between the English and the Wampanoag. This "peace" also included a military alliance should either side be attacked.

Both sides needed this alliance. The Wampanoag had lost many

Massasoit's men kept a close watch on the English settlement. They observed the men, women, and children as they gathered crops and played games in the cleared fields.

people to the plague, and though the English had powerful weapons, there were very few of them. Both sides likely thought that if they joined together they could keep the Narragansett and other more powerful neighboring tribes from taking advantage of their vulnerable position. This agreement was made in March of 1621. Shortly after this meeting, Carver died and was succeeded by William Bradford. It is likely that the English harvest of 1621 was the next occasion that Massasoit traveled to the English town.

Making a Myth

THERE WAS NEITHER CRANBERRY SAUCE nor pumpkin pie at the 1621 harvest celebration. There were no Indians with woven blankets over their shoulders and large feathered headdresses cascading down their backs. There were no Pilgrims in somber black clothes and tall hats with silver buckles, either. The English didn't even call themselves Pilgrims at the time. That's the myth.

The 19th-century painters who created these dramatic images were just plain wrong. They got their ideas about Indian dress from western Plains Indians who performed in Buffalo Bill's Wild West show and from popular "historical" pageants staged by non-Indians. They wanted to show the religious intensity and bravery of the English, looking prosperous and wearing somber clothing. They often drew the Native people to look like ignorant savages, outnumbered by the English and lurking on the sidelines. These images have been reproduced in so many schoolrooms and pageants and illustrations that people think they must be true.

At Plimoth Plantation, a living history museum of 17th-century Plymouth, visitors see staff in carefully researched clothing, wearing doublets and waistcoats in shades of red, yellow, blue, or purple. Visitors are often surprised by how colorful English garments were. They are equally surprised to see beautifully decorated Wampanoag clothing, fashioned from deerskin, elk hide, moose hide, and fur. Thorough scholarship, authentic craftsmanship, and careful attention to all the museum's historical details allow Plimoth Plantation to offer a more accurate picture of the past.

This painting by Jennie Brownscombe is a typical romantic 19th-century image of the English at Plymouth. Such paintings distorted what really happened in 1621.

THE HARVEST

IN DECEMBER OF 1621, colonist Edward Winslow wrote a letter that briefly described the year's harvest. In 1622, this letter was included in a publication describing the beginnings of the new English plantation at Plymouth.

Winslow wrote: "Our harvest being gotten in, our governor sent four men on fowling, that so we might after a special manner rejoice together after we had gathered the fruits of our labors. They four in one day killed as much fowl as, with a little help beside, served the company almost a week. At which time, amongst other recreations, we exercised our arms, many of the Indians coming amongst us, and among the rest their greatest king, Massasoit, with some ninety men, whom for three days we entertained and feasted, and they went out and killed five deer, which they brought to the plantation and bestowed on our governor, and upon the captain and others. And although it be not always so plentiful as it was at this time with us, yet by

---

Four Englishmen go fowling, making their way through the marsh grasses to hunt birds, such as ducks, geese, and swans. ABOVE: A Native man draws his bow while hunting. Massasoit's hunters contributed five deer to the 1621 harvest celebration.

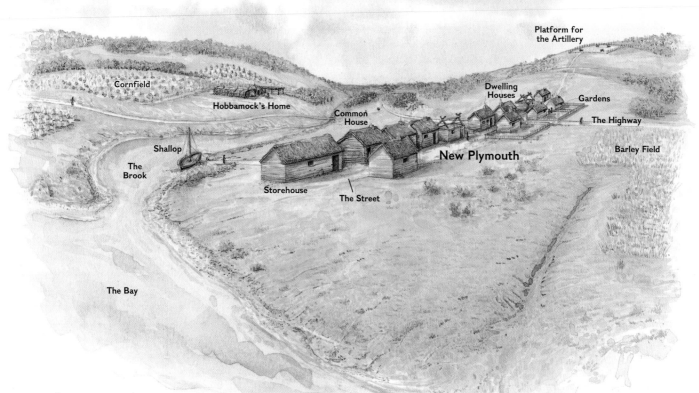

Cornfield

Platform for
the Artillery

Hobbamock's Home

Dwelling
Houses

Common
House

Gardens

Shallop

The Highway

The
Brook

New Plymouth

Barley Field

Storehouse

The Street

The Bay

*Patuxet –
New Plymouth
1621*

the goodness of God, we are so far from want that we often wish you partakers of our plenty."

Over time, Winslow's account of the harvest event has become the basis for the myth of the First Thanksgiving. What actually happened during the three days that English colonists and Wampanoag people met and ate together? First, let's look at some of the events leading up to it.

Tisquantum had been living with the English for almost six months, teaching them how to grow corn and use fish to fertilize their fields. He

and Hobbamock acted as translators and go-betweens for Massasoit.

In early summer, William Bradford sent Edward Winslow and Stephen Hopkins to Pokanoket, the Wampanoag village where Massasoit lived. Tisquantum accompanied them. They brought gifts to Massasoit and, as was customary, they also paid him honor by shooting their muskets in a salute. One of the gifts Bradford sent was a copper chain. Winslow explained that in the future any Native who came to Plymouth carrying the chain would be greeted and entertained as a special messenger from Massasoit.

On the autumn day Winslow described in his letter, when Governor Bradford sent four men to hunt wildfowl, the Wampanoag

A messenger runs to spread the news that Massasoit and his men are approaching (opposite). Governor Bradford (above, center) welcomes Massasoit (above, right) as members of the Wampanoag sachem's entourage look on.

One of the most
persistent myths about
the 1621 celebration
was that it was a
single large meal.
During the three days
that the two cultures
gathered together,
there were many meals
and various other
entertainments.

in the area no doubt heard the shooting. When the Englishmen started marching and firing their muskets in unison, the noise got even louder. It is likely that nearby Native people felt that Massasoit should be informed. Perhaps Massasoit wondered if the English were preparing for war. We may never know, but the fact that he showed up with 90 men, and apparently no women, shows he was being cautious. When it became clear to all that the English were celebrating, Massasoit sent some of his men out to hunt deer for meat to contribute to the feast. Once it was seen to be safe, it is likely that Native women and children, particularly Hobbamock's family, joined them.

For three days, the English and the Native people met and ate together. In English style, Massasoit and his advisers probably ate with the leading men of the colony at a "high table" which featured the best food. Tables were probably set up both indoors and outdoors for the other diners. Men, women, and children all helped in getting and preparing the food. This work included butchering the deer, grinding corn, plucking birds, gathering shellfish, roasting meat, and preparing whatever else was at hand.

Other "entertainments" took place, which probably included playing ball, competitive sports, singing, music, and perhaps even dancing. The Wampanoag were especially fond of games of chance. If the English and Wampanoag children played together, they probably played games known to both cultures, such as blind man's bluff, where a blindfolded "hunter" tries to catch another player, or the ring-and-pin game, where the object is to loop a ring over the pin. The English men took part in "exercising of arms," military drills that involved marching and musket shooting.

Nasaump

NASAUMP IS A TRADITIONAL *WAMPANOAG* DISH which consists of dried corn pounded in a mortar and boiled in plain water to a thick porridge. Usually fruits, such as strawberries, raspberries, or blueberries were added. Another variation included clam broth with native herbs (green onions, wild garlic). The English ate several versions of this dish as well.

YOU WILL NEED:
1 quart water
1½ cups coarse grits or hominy
OPTIONS:
1 cup clam broth and ½ cup chopped green onions OR
        1 cup fresh strawberries, raspberries, or blueberries

Bring the water to a boil in a large pot. Gradually add the hominy, stirring until it comes back to a boil. Turn down the heat to low and cook very gently for 10 minutes, stirring frequently. Remove from the heat and allow to stand one-half to one hour. Before serving, reheat over medium heat, stirring. (If you are adding clam broth and green onions or fruit, you can do so at this point.) The dish can also be reheated in a covered, buttered baking dish in a 350° oven for 45 minutes. You may need to add a bit more water.

INDIGENOUS FOODSTUFFS—foods native to the region—made up the bulk of both the Wampanoag and the English diet. While turkey and pumpkin may have been eaten at the harvest celebration, much of what we now think of as the "traditional" Thanksgiving menu was not available in 1621. If wild turkey were served, it was without cranberry sauce. Potatoes were not grown in New England until the 18th century. Sugar was in short supply, so there were probably very few sweets.

Stewed Pompion
"The Ancient New England Standing Dish"

IN HIS 1672 BOOK *NEW ENGLANDS RARITIES DISCOVERED,* John Josselyn describes "The Ancient New England Standing Dish." The use of the word "ancient" suggests that the first English housewives in New England relied on vast kettles of stewed pumpkin to fill up their families through the fall and winter months. The phrase "standing dish" implies its presence every day, if not at every meal.

YOU WILL NEED:
4 cups of cooked pumpkin or squash (seeded, and steamed or baked),
   roughly mashed
3 tablespoons butter
2 to 3 teaspoons cider vinegar
1 or 2 teaspoons ground ginger
½ teaspoon salt

In a saucepan over medium heat, stir and heat all the ingredients together. Adjust seasonings to taste and serve hot.

GIVING THANKS

1621

MOST LIKELY, THE WAMPANOAG MEN built shelters to stay in for the three days while they visited the English settlement. Other Wampanoag people may have arrived later when they heard about the gathering. The leading men of the Plymouth Colony treated Massasoit as visiting royalty, showing that they respected his power and were grateful for his kindness to them.

The Wampanoag were perhaps there more for political rather than celebratory reasons, but the concept of a harvest gathering was familiar to them. Since long before the arrival of Europeans, the Wampanoag had celebrated festivals of thanks that took place at particular times of the year, including the "Strawberry Thanksgiving" and the "Green Corn Thanksgiving." At these Native festivals, the Creator's gift of food was celebrated with songs, dances, and stories that reminded the People to be generous and grateful. The bounty of the harvest was shared with the community.

Wampanoag men built shelters to sleep in during their three-day stay. ABOVE: Corn was a staple food of the Wampanoag, and they had ceremonies of thanks for it when it was ripe. Native people celebrated many such thanksgivings throughout the year.

Food, including cod, sea bass, venison, duck, clams, cornmeal, beans, squash, nuts, and dried berries, was given away to neighbors to remind the People of their need for and responsibility to one another.

For the English, harvest was the culmination of the year's hard work in the fields. Bountiful crops were a reason to celebrate. In England, these celebrations might be small suppers for individual families. But often neighbors or whole villages joined together to rejoice. The 1621 gathering in Plymouth was not a religious gathering but most likely a harvest celebration much like those the English had known in farming communities back home. The English never once used the word "thanksgiving" in association with their 1621 harvest celebration.

"Thanksgiving" was a term well known to the English, though it was not associated with festivals. Special days of thanksgiving marked by religious services were an important part of English life. The Plymouth colonists brought this tradition with them to New England where it evolved over their years in the colony. The colonists' religious days of thanksgiving involved morning and afternoon services. Worship rather than feasting was the focus of the early thanksgivings.

Although prayers of thanks were probably offered at the 1621 harvest gathering, the first recorded religious thanksgiving day in Plymouth happened in 1623—a full two years later. On this occasion, the colonists were giving thanks to God for rain after a two-month drought. It was not until centuries later that the 1621 harvest gathering would be incorrectly dubbed the First Thanksgiving.

William Bradford offers a prayer before the meal, as was customary for the English. It is likely that the most important men from both cultures dined together.

Evolution of a Holiday

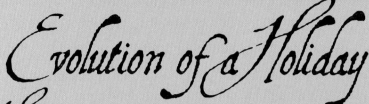

HOW DID A 1621 HARVEST gathering evolve into a popular holiday? Colonists, states, and later the government of the United States, proclaimed special days of thanksgiving for particular occasions. Although without Wampanoag corn, there would have been no harvest to celebrate in 1621, in later years the colonists proclaimed days of thanksgiving for military victories over Native people. One came after the burning of the Pequot fort in 1637. Another celebrated the death of Massasoit's son, at the end of "King Philip's War" in 1676. The first nationwide Thanksgiving celebrated victory over the British at the Revolutionary War Battle of Saratoga in 1777.

In the 19th century the modern Thanksgiving holiday began to take shape. In 1841, New England historians rediscovered the passage about the 1621 harvest gathering and incorrectly labeled it the First Thanksgiving. Then in 1846 Sarah Josepha Hale, editor of a magazine called *Godey's Lady's Book,* began to campaign for an annual national Thanksgiving holiday.

In 1863, during the Civil War, President Abraham Lincoln declared two national Thanksgivings. One, in August, commemorated the Battle of Gettysburg. The second, in November, was to give thanks for "general blessings." During this time of turmoil, the myth of brave Pilgrims inviting Native people to sit with them in community and peace was very comforting. The autumn date coincided with New England's seasonal harvests and soon became adopted as a general Thanksgiving Day.

These popular images show the turkey as the classic symbol of the American holiday of Thanksgiving.

A Broken Peace

*F*OR THREE DAYS IN 1621, Massasoit, Bradford, and the people they led celebrated the harvest together. They felt safe in the assurance of the agreement between them. But Massasoit's alliance with the Plymouth colonists would last for only a single generation. By 1640, the political situation in New England had changed. In 1630 the population of Plymouth Colony was 300. By the end of the decade it was close to 2,000. Demand for land led to disputes among the colonists and between colonists and Native people. Tensions arose that lasted for decades and still linger today.

After the 1637 massacre of Pequot at Mystic Fort, New England's Native people began to form broader alliances. In 1675 Massasoit's son, Metacom, also called Philip, rallied people from many Native nations in an attempt to drive the English out of Native homelands. During "King Philip's War," many English and Wampanoag died. English settlements were burned. Native captives were sold into slavery in the West Indies. By the war's end in 1676, Metacom had been killed and his nine-year-old son enslaved. The Wampanoag had lost their political independence and much of their homeland. The town of Plymouth declared a special day of thanksgiving for the English victory.

Considering this history and what came in later centuries, Native people do not share in the popular reverence for the traditional New England "Thanksgiving." To the Wampanoag, the holiday is a reminder of the arrival of the English in their homeland, a presence that brought betrayal and bloodshed. Since 1970, many Native people have gathered at the statue of Massasoit in Plymouth, Massachusetts, each Thanksgiving Day. They keep a vigil in memory of the struggles of their ancestors and the strength of Wampanoag persistence.

English muskets, used for hunting, were also weapons of war.
By the 1630s, as the English wanted more land, tensions developed
with Native people. In 1675, a full-scale war broke out.

BRINGING THE PAST TO LIFE

IN THE 20TH CENTURY, people have begun to reexamine American history. Efforts have been made to think in new ways about how we became the nation we are today.

Interpreter Marietta Mullen trades her 21st-century clothes for a 17th-century outfit when she goes to work on Mayflower II. *She also adopts a 17th-century English dialect.*

This means that many untold stories are now coming to light. One of these is the story of the harvest at Plymouth in 1621.

In October 2000, several hundred people gathered at the modern-day Plimoth Plantation museum to reenact the 1621 harvest gathering. For three days, photographers, advisers, Plimoth Plantation staff, and members of the Wampanoag Nation and other Native communities came together to depict the events of that time. This event, a first in the history of the museum, turned out to be a powerful gathering for all involved.

In preparation for the weekend, six Native artisans worked with deerskin, furs, beads, bone, shell, feathers, and other natural materials to handcraft traditional decorated garments for the Native participants to wear. Many local Wampanoag people proudly wore these garments in memory of their ancestors and in honor of all their relatives who are still here, living in Wampanoag territory. In the end, over a hundred Wampanoag and other Native people participated in the event, including more than 90 Native men. The Wampanoag people, and those from other Native nations who assisted them, felt an enormous sense of pride in seeing their community acknowledged, celebrated, and portrayed so respectfully and so beautifully.

The Wampanoag Indian Program at Plimoth Plantation has become a gathering place where Wampanoag artisans, scholars, performers, and educators actively work to recover and interpret the history and culture of their ancestors. The Wampanoag Indian Program has brought back many crafts and skills that have not been practiced for a century or longer.

Historians reinterpret the documents, artifacts, and oral histories about the early days of the colony, in an effort to replace popular myths with accurate history. A museum that started as a place to commemorate the Pilgrims has become a place where the understanding of history is being corrected to include all perspectives of the past. The photographs that appear in this book show some of the people who worked together to make that history come to life.

In the 1627 Village, role-players go about the daily activities of the English community. Becky Noonan, a costumed role-player, laughs with the visitors.

At the Wampanoag Indian Program education site (shown above) and at Hobbamock's Homesite, visitors have the chance to talk to Native staff about the history, culture, and traditions of the Wampanoag people.

Chronology

ANCIENT WAMPANOAG HISTORY

13,500 – 8000 years ago: For 10,000 years before European contact, after the last ice age, Native people inhabited the area we now call New England. They hunted mastodon, caribou, deer, bear, and other animals and birds, and fished in lakes, rivers, and the sea. Fruits, nuts, berries, leafy plants, barks, and roots provided food and medicine. Shelters, woven mats, and household goods were constructed from wood, bark, and grasses.

8000 – 1000 years ago: After the corn plant was first cultivated in Mexico, it spread through trade networks across the continent. About 2,000 years ago, Wampanoag people started growing corn and beans. Seasonal and monthly community celebrations gave thanks for the bounty of the land.

EUROPEAN CONTACT AND THANKSGIVING DAYS

1000 – 1700: European explorers, goods, and diseases entered northeastern Native communities.

1524 – 1614: Explorers of Cape Cod included Giovanni da Verrazanno (1524), Bartholomew Gosnold (1602), Martin Pring (1603), Samuel de Champlain (1605), and John Smith (1614).

1611 – 1614: English Captain Edward Harlow captured five Native men and brought them back to England. Captain Thomas Hunt captured Wampanoag men: 20 from Patuxet, including Tisquantum (Squanto), and seven from Nauset, to sell as slaves in Spain.

1616 – 1620: Several epidemics of European disease hit the northeast. In 1618 Tisquantum returned to his homeland on an English ship.

November 11, 1620: The *Mayflower* made landfall at what is now Provincetown. In late December the passengers decided to settle at the then empty village site of Patuxet, renamed New Plymouth.

March – August 1621: Samoset visited the Plymouth settlement and brought Tisquantum, who stayed with the English. Massasoit and Governor Carver made a treaty. Hobbamock moved to Plymouth.

Mid-September – early-November, 1621: Sometime in this period, the Pokanoket and other Wampanoag met with the colonists for a three-day harvest celebration.

July 26, 1623: The English colonists observed a religious day of thanksgiving in response to the end of a drought and the safe arrival of more colonists from England.

August 1623: Massasoit, four other sachems, and 120 Wampanoag men were invited to William Bradford's wedding.

1624 – 1636: Trade, settlement, and conflict increased. Plymouth Colony established trading houses on the Kennebec and Penobscot Rivers in Maine. More English settled Massachusetts Bay Colony. John Pynchon set his trading house at Matianuck (Windsor, CT) on the Connecticut River. Roger Williams founded Providence Plantation (Rhode Island).

July 1637: Soldiers under Captain John Mason and Captain John Underhill burned the Pequot fort on the Mystic River; 700 Pequot men, women, and children were killed and the survivors were sold into slavery. The colony of Connecticut observed a day of thanksgiving; Massachusetts Bay Colony set aside October 12 as a day of thanksgiving "to God for subduing the Pequots."

1650 – 1663: Ministers began efforts to convert the Wampanoag to Christianity. Thomas Mayhew built a church on Martha's Vineyard. Native translators and printers worked with John Eliot to publish the Bible in the Wampanoag language.

June 1675 – August 12, 1676: During "King Philip's War," Massasoit's son, Metacom, led a rebellion against the colonists. Many Native people were killed or sold into slavery in the West Indies. Shortly after Metacom's death, Plymouth declared August 12 as a day of public thanksgiving for the English victory.

1680s – 1770s: Colonial governors proclaimed periodic days of thanksgiving, often in late autumn.

November 1, 1777: The first national Thanksgiving Day was declared by the Continental Congress after the American victory over the British at Saratoga. The actual celebration was December 18.

1770s – 1840s: Thanksgiving days, which still varied from state to state, were occasions for feasting, military parades, shooting matches, and public proclamations that recalled the trials of the "Pilgrim Fathers."

1846: Sarah Josepha Hale, editor of *Godey's Lady's Book,* began her campaign for a national Thanksgiving Day, to fall on the last Thursday of November.

August 6, 1863: President Abraham Lincoln declared a day of Thanksgiving for Union victories in the Civil War. He declared a second Thanksgiving Day in late November for "the blessings of fruitful field."

1864 – present: The traditional American Thanksgiving Day has been celebrated every year since 1863. Originally the last Thursday of November, the time was amended to the fourth Thursday in 1942.

1970 – present: Each Thanksgiving Day, many Native people meet at the statue of Massasoit in Plymouth, Massachusetts, to observe a National Day of Mourning.

October 2000: Several hundred people, including over a hundred Wampanoag and other Native people, gathered at Plimoth Plantation to reenact the 1621 harvest gathering.

Index

Illustrations are indicated by **boldface.**

Bibliography

FURTHER READING ABOUT NATIVE TRADITIONS

Circle of Thanks: Native American Poems and Songs of Thanksgiving, by Joseph Bruchac, illustrated by Murv
    Jacob (Bridgewater Books, 1996)
Giving Thanks: A Native American Good Morning Message by Chief Jake Swamp, illustrated by Erwin Printup,
    Jr. (Lee & Low, 1995)
Giving Thanks: The 1621 Harvest Feast, by Kate Waters, photographs by Russ Kendall (Scholastic Press, 2001)
Tapenum's Day: A Wampanoag Indian Boy in Pilgrim Times, by Kate Waters, photographs by Russ Kendall,
    (Scholastic Press, 1996)
The Wampanoag and the First Thanksgiving, (Everyday Learning Corp., 1997)

TEACHER MATERIAL

Thanksgiving: A Native Perspective, written and compiled by Doris Seale, Beverly Slapin, Carolyn Silverman
    (Oyate, 1998)
Through Indian Eyes: The Native Experience in Books for Children, edited by Beverly Slapin, Doris Seale
    (Oyate, 1998)
Wampanoag: People of the East (Plimoth Plantation, 1999)
Journey to the New World (Plimoth Plantation, 1999)
Life in 1627 Plymouth (Plimoth Plantation, 1999)

PRIMARY SOURCE MATERIAL

Of Plymouth Plantation 1620-1647, by William Bradford, edited by Samuel Eliot
    Morison (Alfred A. Knopf, 1952)
Good Newes From New England, by Edward Winslow, 1624, (Applewood Books, reprint)
Mourt's Relation: A Journal of the Pilgrims at Plymouth 1622, edited by Dwight B. Heath
    (Applewood Books, reprint 1963)
Three Visitors to Early Plymouth, edited by Sydney V. James (Plimoth Plantation, 1963)

Further resources available by visiting www.plimoth.org

For my niece and nephew Maeve and Isaac O'Neill and their Native ancestors — COG
To the ancestors and to the young ones — MMB
To Saskia and Calder — SB & CC

ACKNOWLEDGMENTS: Our thanks to the staff of the Wampanoag Indian Program at Plimoth Plantation, especially Linda Coombs, Darrel Wixon, the WIP Artisans, Nancy Eldredge and Darius Coombs; to Jessie Little Doe Fermino and Martin Hendricks; and the members of the Wampanoag Nation and other Native communities, including Narragansett, Nipmuc, Mohegan, Cherokee, Lakota, Aymara, Quechua, Montagnais, and Navajo for their participation in the recreation that allowed this story to be told. We also acknowledge the staff of Plimoth Plantation, especially Stuart Bolton, Carol City, Kathleen Curtin, Jill Hall, John Kemp, Liz Lodge, Kathy Roncarati, Maureen Richard, Carolyn Travers, and Lisa Whalen. Special thanks to Peggy Baker at the Pilgrim Hall Museum for her generous loan of Thanksgiving artifacts from her private collection.

ILLUSTRATIONS CREDITS: pp. 26–27 Courtesy of the Pilgrim Society, Plymouth, Massachusetts; pp. 40–41 Courtesy of Peggy Baker, private collection

ISBN 0-439-46276-2

12 11 10 9 8 7 6 5   4 5 6 7/0

Printed in the U.S.A.   40

First Scholastic printing, November 2002

The text of this book is set in Garamond.
The display text is Aquiline and Chanson d'Amour.